A Weasel in the Works

Book Six of the Weasel Chronicles

by Ken S Green

To order additional copies of this book, contact:
Xlibris
844-714-8691
www.Xlibris.com
Orders@Xlibris.com

ISBN: Softcover   978-1-6641-6596-0
       Hardcover   978-1-6641-6597-7
       EBook   978-1-6641-6595-3

Print information available on the last page

Rev. date: 08/31/2021

★ OTHER CHARACTERS ★

Ah mr Weasel .. welcome back .. thanks ever so much for my What Knot Award ... that was really a really good story about the Weasel Without A Cause ... and i really read *all* of it ... i'm so proud of myselves ... but it *was* really stupid, wasn't it ? ... unless ... did i miss something there ? ... no ... no ... i got it all ... and those new tails that you threaten to tell us all all about sound *really* dumb too, eh ? ... so wouldn't it be best to rest a bit now ? ... you have been underwhelmed by a lot of stress lately ... now what i would do is sit back ... relax about ... look out the window ... sip some nice icy liquid Weasolene (TM) on the rocks .. while you tell us about some different other cartoon characters just for the fun of it ... aha ha ... its is so easy ... just unshackle the brain cells from the old Weasel ... and ... well, there you have it ...

Wha ? ... *other* cartoon characters ?? .. there you have it ? ... wha ? ... unshackle ? ... wha? ... stoopid ? ... wha? ... what ? ... sniff ... am i art so unappreciated ?? .... grrr ... gets right up my nose ... sniff ... how did this happen ?? ... hadn't i just been in the office run as number one Weasel ?? .. before i zippered out of the picture when last seen in the last scene ?? .. what is this ??? WHO is This ??

It's me, Author !! Author ??

★ STILL NUMBER ONE ★

Now, now, don't take it so hard .... i didn't mean other characters as in no more Weasel ... but perhaps ... maybe ... some of Weasel's ... *friends* ... friends he hasn't, like, introduced us to yet because he has been too busy hogging the limelite ... those other ones ... they could never take his place ... Weasel is still and always will be ... number one ...

What ? ... hogging the limelight ??? .... moi ??? .... what *are* you saying, Author ???? ...

★ WHAT A CARD ★

Oh that Weasel .... what a card ...

A card ? ... you say ? ... hmm ... yes, okay, then ... pick one, you !!

★ PICKY A CARD ★

Hummmm .... which card ?... let me think ... ok, the light red one ... second in from the left ....

Ah the old second in from the left ploy ... hmmm ... let's see ... now ... oh ... i am sorry ... you picked the NO of Clubs ... well never mind ... better luck next time, Author ...

★ FOUR CARDS ★

★ THE RED ONE ★

Okay ... okay ... i'll take the ... uh ... the ... uh ... the red card .... yes yes that's the one for meeeeee ...

The red card ... you want the red one ... oh ... gee ... bummer ... you picked the NAW of Diamonds ... well we can't win 'em all ... can we now ? ...

★ THREE CARDS ★

Hummm ... okay the light violetishy one on the end at the right ... i'll take that one then ... i have the right to win something ... give me something .... gimmmmeeeeee.....

And he wants the violetishy one ... well ... okay ...

★ BROKEN HEART ★

Oh my my my my me oh my ... the NOPE of Hearts ... terrible fortune lands uponst thee, Author ... a broken heart ... but that was a good guess ... a fine nice try ... but you can not take nice trys to the bank, now, can we ? ... so ... how many cards are left ? ... let's see ...

★ 50 FIFTY CHANCE ★

Well, let me see then .... two left ... i have a 50/50 chance ... i can't loose now ... the odds are on my side .... okay ... i'll take the one on the right looking out ... no no ! ... look out ! ... yes ... gimmmeee that which is mine .... gimmeee the prize .... oh yes, i want it ... all that i deserve ....

And they want the one on my right ... so it is time to choose off which you think is the stinkiest wink ... whooz time has come up to it ? ... which card gets punched ? ... whom's lights are out ? ...

★ NICE TO BE NICE ★

Oh yes ... me ... me ... me ... i'm the one to win ... gimmmeee my prize ...... i neeed to win .... come on, you can do it .... lets you be fair ... let me win ..... remember, "it's so nice to be nice" ......

Huh ? ... but ... but ... this is ... you have chosen ... you picked the NOT of Spades ! ... oh dear this is not nice at all ... is this all that you deserve ? ... the gimmmeee to you ? ... the prize with which it is yer belief to be yorn ? ... well ... do not despair ... perhaps you could dig in the garden with it ... ?

★ ONE CARD ★

Hey whom turned on the lights ??? ... well, no matter ... there's just only one card left ...

★ AND THE WINNING CARD IS ★

No, no ... yes ... there is one more card ... i still get to choose ... i'll take the last card ... yes, yes ... that is my choice ... the last card is the one i want .... the one i really wanted all along ... so now i choose it ... and now i can win because the odds are more in my favour you see ? .... you do understand ? ... yes, of course you do .... so now gimmmeeeeee my prize ! .... yes, *my* prize that is rightly *mine* .... all that i truly deserve i will have now .... finally by the process of elimination i have narrowed it down to the winning card .... i win ... hoooorrrraaaaaaaaayyyyyyyyyyyyyyyyyy!!!!!!!!!!!!!!!!

But ....

Yes, that is what i said ... that is the card i want ... the winning card !!!! .... now i can have all that i deserve all that i have coming to me ... the Big One ... the prize of prizes .... give it to me ..... nowwwwwww ... no more delay ... cash equivalents are also good if the prize is too bulky to send ..... gimmmee ... gimmmeeee .... gimmmmeeeeee .....

Dim the lights pleeze ... thank yew ... but ... hey wait a minute ... this can't be right ...

★ ASK THE AUDIENCE ★

No buts about it ... there were five to begin with ... i have chosen four ... that means that the card in your paw is the *one* .... there can be only one ... the card that will give me my fortune .... the Winning Card ... the fifth card ... so don't try and weasel out of it ..... five minus four is one .... the math cannot be denied ... so let's have it ... no more delays, no more paws ... let's get that valuable prize to meeee ... asappppppp .... oh i can hear my bank account groaning when i go and deposit all that cash equivalent all at once ..... yesss ... gimmmmeeeeeeeeeeeee it to meeeeeeee ......

Well ... this is an unusual dilemma ... i think we better ask the audience on this one ... mykrofon please ... thank yew ... and can we have the spot light over there ? ... yes ... yes ... you there ... the one with the ears ...

9

It is the Winning Card ... my prize .... send me my prize ... i've already explained it for you .... there were five cards and i chose four ... and that leaves the last one, which i choose .... and it is the winning card .... so i get the big one .... the *jackpot* .... the big kahchoogna ... the folding green stuff ... the large denomination notes ... yesss .... i'm rich .... i'm rich .... role me in the dough ... gimmmmeeeeeeeeeeeeee my well deserved reward ....

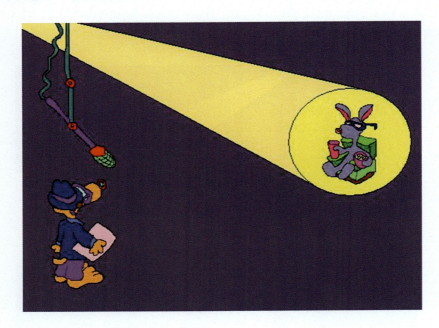

Ah yes ... Hush, hush now Author ... here we are ... mister Blue Bunny with the ears, i am sure, we can presume ... and we can presume, i am sure, that you know the story ... having been sitting there in the audience with those listening ears and all, for the duration since the doors have been tightenedly closed for the show ... in mine paw here i am holding what could very well be *the* Winning Card ... or is it ? ... i will show you to it ... and you must cast a decision over it ... just give us a aye or an nay sign ... but remember ... if you wear dark coloured spectacles ... a wink is *not* as good as a nod ... for obvious reasons ...

Audience ? ... audience ? ... there's no reason to ask no stupid audience ... i won ... i am the winner ... the guy who got it right ... i get it ... you are just stahlling arn't you ? ... don't think you can pull the wool/cotton/elastic blend over my eyes you, you, you ... Weasel, you ! .... but i must calm down for this cannot be good for my blood pressure .... i'll just take a few deeeeep breathes and try again ... gasp ... gulp ... wheeze ..... there, now i am calm....

Oh ... what a reaction ... dear my golly ... this does not look good ... a hopping mad rabbit ... well ... we better just file away this vote ... and now let's let us see what some other less bouncy characters have to think ... no hasty decisions can be made with such an important matter as the *Winning Card* ...

Hello ?.... yes, that is correct, no hasty decisions ... i am the winner so naturally the prize ... that which i so rightly deserve .... is mine .... yes, mine ... all mine .... it is precious ... *my precious* ... send it to me now .... you are falling slowly asleep ... my words are penetrating your ears ... you will send me my prize ... yes, now ... go and call the bank ... see how easy it is ? ... direct electronic transfer .... yes, that is goooooooooodddddd......

And here are some fine feathery friends we can ask ... okay ... okay ... okay ! ... stop shoving ! ... get in the proper pecking order ! ... ya'll will all get a chance to see the card and cast a vote ... equal opportunity uber all of us ... now calm down with the feathers and the beaks ... stop trying to play tricksies on me ! ...

Tricksies ? ... no no you are wrong ... it is all in your mind ... relax now and take a deep breath ... don't you feel better now ? ... gooood ... now i want you to close your eyes and drift away ... but not too far away ... you may need to reach your checkbook ... yes, there you are ... comfortable aren't you ? ... okay now just listen to my voice ... i am the winner of the prize ... breathe, breathe ... yes, that is good ... relax ... i am the winner of the prize because i chose the right card ... yes, yes ... i know i had to choose five of five before i got there, but that doesn't matter now, does it ? ... just relax and empty your mind of all senseless protest ... yes, now ... tell the birds to be dismissed ... it was all a silly mix up ... shift the spotlight back on yourself and then announce the news to the waiting world ... i am the winner of the prize ... yes, see how good that feels ?... all mine ... not yours, mine ... yes, you are doing well ... announce away ...

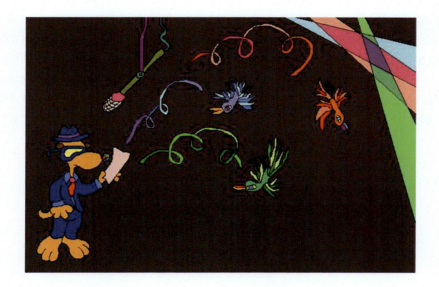

What is all that mumbling noise in the background ? ... the prize is mine ? ... will no whom rid me of this meddling sound ? ... this *static* ... this Author ? ... let's see now ... hey, you birdies look at this !! ... hmmm ... well ... this is not looking so very promising well either ... quite flipping shocking actually ... so far all we have had is some quite unfavourable responses ... and some very negative bird feedback, too ... tusk tusk ... the Winning Card is not meant for *we know whom*, of course ... however there are still some more possibly less flighty characters to consider this question with ... and we will ask them, coming up after this brief message ... sit tight, Weasel be right back ! ...

This is insult !!! ... first rabbit and now bird !!! .... i tell you clearly now feelthy vermin, that i am winner of contest ... take away bird and stop play about and send me prize .... what? ... oh sorry, didn't realize i am on air ... hello ... hello ... there has obviously been some mistake, possibly an oversight by the Awards Committee ... shouldn't be anything that can't be rectified with a little switch ... just flick the correct switch and the money will be on its way into my account ... you of course will appreciate that it will make me very happy to accept the prize that i have won don't you ? ... so, enough with the audience ... no more rabbits, no more birds, just prize .... yes ? ... there is no need to go *anywhere* or to be right back ... or to be commercial ... the world is already too commercial ...

Ah ... there you are, noise maker ... listen ... here is your answer ... *NO* !! ... okay ? ... now, pleased to be quiet ... okay ... hush ... now let's just leave pleonasms behind for a non prolix moment and get down to the nitty witty gritty and listen up ... are you in a slightly refractory recusant type mood ? ... do you want to make a frutescent fashion statement without seeming frumpy ? ... you want your privacy in a nice privet of where the public is not privy of ? ... where you can get some peace and rasta from the furious world and be on yourn own for a while ? ... well, of course you do ... but you know what they say about ... they say a lot about ... and one thing they say about is ... no Weasel is a island ... eh ? ...

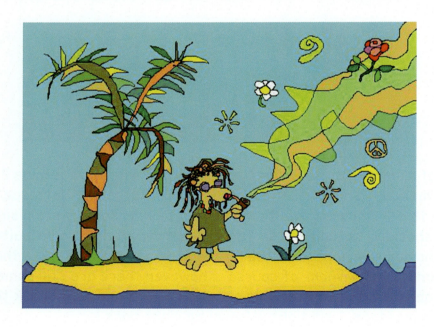

Yeah shore mon ... well they say all too much about everything ... eh ? ... okay ... ganja knows weed agree ... no Weasel *is* a island ... okay ya ? ... but now you can *Rent* one ... or Rent to Own ... or just Own to Own ... to Rent or rant or root or rastaboot on or whatever you choose to want to do ... easy terms ... we accept plastic per say per usual ... unless it washes up on the beach, then it is returned pronto ... so please send all your card and bank and personal info to :

RastaWeasel
Noweaselseneyelsore Box RU1
Weasel Internatural Mail Post Delivery Forwarding Service
Freeweaseltowne, closed by mainland Weaslton,
Boweashamburglian Islands
Weast Oceanic Weaslonia SNEW by NEWS 4

and wheel fix you right up, down and around with your very own wee island ... custom designed for your every needs ... location, location, location they say ... so how about around right about *here* for your location ? ... and thank yew ever so very much ... Enjoy !!

★ Jaws One And Two ★

What is this ? ... all i want is my prize ... what kind of outfit are you people running ? ... some hairy little who-knows-what smoking some i-doubt-that's-tobacco standing on some beach assuming that i care about renting a island to own ... what ever happened to that little fancy guy with the card ? ... with my card ... the Winning Card ... where is he ? ... i wasn't finished with him yet ... this is getting too difficult ... but i can go the distance ... because i know, yes i know ... that the Prize Grande is mine ... i have the time you see ... oh ... there he is ... now, be a good fellow and return to the question at hand ... about what actually the quickest way to transfer robust sums of cash into my account de banco is ...

Well ... fine ... here are a couple of guys whom are a bite more down to earth so to speak ... shall we refer to them two as Jaws one and two ? ... let's see what they have to think upon the matter of concern, which is the Winning Card ...

★ Waters The Matter ★

No, no, no .... it is easier than this .... perhaps you did not understand earlier ... there is no need to consult anyone or body at all ... no rabbits ... no birds ... no nasty fishies ... no nothing or none more ... think of the logic .... 5 cards ... 4 are chosen and are not the Winning Card ... that leaves one card in your paw that has got to be the Winning Card .... and since i now choosed the last card, that means that i am entitled to the Big Prize ... this is the famous Weasel With Five in the Hand Contest ? ... big money, prize chances ? ... sooooo, pleeaaassse stop all this now and gimmmeeeee the prize so that i can be on my way .....

Hey ... waters the matter ? ... flippin fish sticks ... i just showed you the winning card ... that's all ... there's no need to flipper out about it ... fiddle flounders ... well ... we certainly are getting nowhere this way ... hmmm ... now which whom can we ask about with now ? ...

Oh wait come back ... why have you swum away ? ... give your opinion, say something ... this irritating rodent-like creature is withholding a vast fortune that rightly belongs to me ... for it is i who chose the Winning Card ... the one in his paw ... i want my prize ...

Hey, you up there ! ... the one with the lights ! ... what whom are you ? ... are you mano or mouseo ? ... come down i have something to show you ... something you must see ... i need your opinion ... donna be afraid ... its all right now ... i've learned my lesson well ... you see you canna please everywhich whom ... so you gotta please your Weasel ... that's me ... and i'm alright now jack ... i feel good like i know about wood ... so good ... spruced up ... come on ... its just a card ... could be *the* winning card ... need to hear from you ... get your tail down here now ! ... or i'll unplug your lights out ! ...

Enough !!!! ... i can't stand it any more ... it has been much too too long now ... maybe more ... i want my prize ... why do you keep torturing me ??? who is that stupid pink eared mouse any way?? the audience didn't answer and the fish didn't answer ... so by default and it is no one's fault, the prize is mine ... mine do you hear alllll mine ... now calm down and announce the winner for all the world to hear ... It's ME, Author !! .. and be quick about it !!

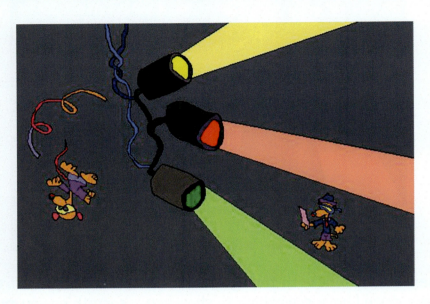

Ah yes ... comey come here mousey ... looky look down at the card ... just a glance'll do it ... yes, you see it? what ? ... hello ? ... another bad reaction, an oopsy daisy over double dual back flip ? ... aren't we just over doing it a smidge ? ... this is so negativish ... can this really be *the* Winning Card if it causes such reactions as this ? ... well ... as i look about myself and around here, i don't see any other cards ... so by processing illuminated deletions, that means ... gee ... it must be the Winning Card ... but, then, why can't i get a reliable second opinion ? ...

It is at times like this, these difficult times ... this historical unveiling and de-mystifying of the mysterious *Winning Card* ... when all Weasel, friends and company must gather under the spot light of the Great Weasel in the Sky and confer in faith and scrutiny on this matter ... so come now, look lively, we're on prime mordial time here ... lets all have a big group hug ... everywhom and whozit too ...

What is this? insolent young pup ... continuing without benefiting meeee with the prize that is mine .... yes, all mine !! .. send it to me by registered post ... better yet, charter a jet and have it delivered to meeee in person as quickly as possible .... get the prize that is so rightly mine ... that which i deserve .... to meee now !!

Yes ... everybody, just ignore that ranting pleading noise in the background ... yes ... ja so ... all together now ... positive energy ... i can feel it resonating ... Uhmmmm ... Ohmmmm ... Chant together ... Rah Mon ! ... Rah Mon ! ... Go Go Go Mon ! ... Hoo Rah Mon ! ... Who Rah Mon ? ... Rah Mon Whom Nose Everything Mon ? ... hey ! ... whose nose *is* in my ear, mon ? ... Uhmmmm ? ...

★ True Pipe Dream Reality ★

Ach and what a pretty picture life could be ... all whoms living in harmony ... without the harm ... but plenty of mony ... how happy we all would be ! ... but shall we leave this idyllic picture for a moment and just pop into some true pipe dream reality ? ... and think humbly upon that which we are searching for ...

No wait ! ... let us try a simple mantra instead ... now sit comfortably and breathe deeply ... repeat after me until it becomes a natural steady flow of breathe and words .... you will feel better ... i will feel richer ... i mean better ... oohme wannagive tohe whohas won .... oohme wannagive tohe whohas won ... to be won with one who has won one big won ... see ? ... can you feel the unity with the universe ?? ... it feels better to give ... i feel better to receive .... transfer that which is so rightly mine to me .. and the world will be a better place and have a sunny face, too ... it's so nice to be nice you know ...

So sorry ... can no wait now, for we must move on towards that which all of us seek ... a little plot of grass with perhaps a peace of security and respectable good health and, may as well, toss in a few zillion gold Spanish florins from the lost treasures of the Sierra Madre and Padres ... simple things like ... like ... like ... eh ? ... oops, what is this then, what comes my way uponst a fair breeze ? ... am i a dreamer or a pipe dream ? ... is the pipe dreaming me ? ... what *is* realty, really ? ...

Ah ha, a card ... a card is reality ... indeed, it is so ... but what is the significance of yonder card here and where did it come from, a Nutter story, perhaps ? ... well, anyway, let's see, hmmm ... yes, yes ... yes ... ah ha ... i know what this is, it is a *Winning Card* ... but oh ! ... oh, i see, now that i look at it, hmmm ... no, no ... yes, definitely no ... it is not a *Winning Card* ... usually i think not "much" ... however, when i do, i think much "not" ... and i think much "not" now ... definitely not now ! ... not, not thinking ... but thinking "*not*" very much ... i think "not" ... it can'tst be, you know ... somewhom's not playing with a full deck around aboutst here ... i had better just give the card back ... yes ... i think not to keep it now ... away with it ... it must be tossed about and away ...

How is it possible that such a simple operation ... that is, the handing over of the prize to it's rightfully won winner ... can cause such chaos ??? ... it is scandalous ... and quite frankly, disturbing too ... why throw the Card away when the answer lies within your hand ... why try to pass on the inevitable ??? ... it is after all a faktum veritae, a truthful fact ... a faktum absolutum, an absolute truth ... that i have won the awardable, the presentable, the giveable ... yes, it is mine now ... just the simple act of transferring ownership from your organization to me is all that needs to be fulfilled ...

★ Fine Feathered Friends ★

I tossed a card into the air, but wherest it will fall, i know not where ...

Oh ... it t'will fall amongst our fine feathered friends again, it seems ...

★ The Wild Blue Over Yonder ★

Oh, fair plumaged fellows ! ... t'what is this ? ... is this any which way to behave over a Winning Card ? ...

Especially since it is mine own card .. not yours any which way !!

T'we hope not ... t'we'll tweet the whistle on this one ... oops ... too late ... beak on off y'all !... oops .. yonder card is oft to the wild blue sea over yonder, again ...

And so camest yonder card right out of the blue ... to landst once against inst the deep blue, see ? ...

T>where a feeding frenzy t>wert in deep progress .... so, heedless to sayings, yon card did>st not last longer in yonder deep blue than it had>d up in the wild blue yonder ... and the splishing of the splashings and the splashing of the splishings carried it to shore ...

For shore !! For shore !! ... Because it belongs not to dumb fisheses anyway .. it's is mine !!

Where it came to rest undertoe of one of a wee pair of two goody two feet of one of the tribes gals of the Good Summery Tans tribe ... luckily, as usual, the Bad Summery Tans were out to lunch at some nasty dive ... she picked the card upside down and stared at it ... until it made more sense to turn it downside up, which she did ...

And although the word wast writ on the card ... and the word wast sewn verily quiet and clearly ... she read of the word upon the card but understood of it not much, if at all ... and yea .. so it wasp that even as the word were'd writ as the *winning card* ... it got tossed again.... and camest not to bear fruition ....

How could the bear verily sew any fruitations ?? .. It is not bearable for any who but meee !!! .. Why waste the time of day like this ?? .. Just gimme and go away !!

And it beared no fruitations because … the card tumbled onto the sand which was abrasive in between the suits and not at all suitable ground for the settling of a winning card … so, from whence, hence card bounced thence away and downhill onto the rocks … where all wast unsuited for rooting …

Because, the card was on a roll … and continued to … until it came to rest near solid soil by the Fertile Crescent … which some call the Cradle of Civilization …but which is most oft referred to it as the Far Out House where one goes to think … and here it was finally discovered anew by …. do you know which whom ? … The wonderer of wonders it was !!

It makes no matter in a hoot to whom discovered the anew .. It is all bedside the point .. Giving it to me !!

★ The Moment ★

Yes ... it was Moi ... Le Weasel ... your host for tonight ... and wise as i am 'n' was ... i recognized yonder card ... and rescued it from a terrible fate and saved it for reading on a later date ... which is ... now, now, now ... let's be patient ...

And now ... the moment you've all been waiting for, is Now !! ... the announcement of the Winning Card winner ... it is the ... the ... the ...

No, no .. No the the ... the the's right here Baboo ... we already know it is for meee ...

The ... the ... why of course !! ... what else could it be ? ... now we know what all the flipping flipping out was all about ! ... after all these great suspenders have built up and up to this point .. and are just about to snap around to near tumbling ... after all the intrigue and mystery has woven itself into tight twine and is about to come unraveling ... after all this and more ... we now have our answer ... *the* Winning Card for the Big Prize of lots and lots ... for which there can be only One ... one whom to take the wins ... and now we know ... its ... the ... drum roll please ... the ... uh, can we have a zoom close up here ... yes, thanks ... and it's the ... the ... the ...

the ... the ... WEASJOKELER ... ?!

Huh ? ... Wha .. wha ... what ???!!

It took a moment to sink ... then ... i got to get it ... what an honor ... Hooray !! ... there is *no* winning whom ! ... everybody loses !! ... nobody gets it !! .. get it ? ... its so fitting, its apt !!! ... there was a Weasel in the Works all along !!!! ... isn't that just appropriated ?? ... see ? ... the Weasel gets it ! ... it was all just one big Weasjokeler !! ...hey ... don't blame me ... it was the Weasel ... uh huh ... in the *works* ... sav-vy ? ... the Weasel got it ... comprehen-do ? ... hmmm ... hey ...

I thought for a minute ... Oh yeah ! ... i get it ! ... the Weasel got it ! ... *i'm* the Weasel ... i *got* it ! ... yeah ... kool ... hey, why are you all wonderful people looking at *me* like that ? ... now hold onto a minute for a second ... it's not my fault ... i didn't *ask* to be the commonweaseltator for this program, you know ! ... i just helped to stack the deck and rig the show up ... i didn't expect to *win* ...

Huh ?? Huh ?? ... Huuuuhh ???!!

★ TARGETED ★

It was thrust upon me ... it was my destiny, it was ... honest ... they unloaded the dice on me right from the start ... what could i do ? ... i got rolled on a lucky street for a change ... not on a major rue, or anything, just a wee roulette ... besides, i was really only on my way to the fridge for a nibble ... when i was thrust upon with these cards for choosing ... well, my word ! ... my words were not being well received ... i could see there was no point talking at this crowd ...

If you are not believing in what i am telling you about, i announced ... then i must just cash in my paw ... i had a grand paw, after all ... for every paw's a winner, and every paw's a loser ... and the best that you can hope for is to dine in your sleepy cafe ... or ... at least pick up your steaks ... and clear on out of here before i got broke even with a bandana split ... bye now ... thanks for tuning in, all ... geeze ! ... the way ya'll are behaving ... yar should be ashamed of yourselves truly ... but by now and then, the fruit was flying ! ... and i was targeted ...

Dine in your sleepy café ?? You think ?? You sneak .. you, you Weasel !! I'll get you for this !!...

But why ?? ... i quickly grabbed hatten card and re-read the script in case there had been a mistake mistakenly inserted somewhere ... let's see now ... what's the buzz ? ... *fruit flies and Weasel fleas* ... quite buzzy ... this all seemed like a familiar event that I had gone through in some long forgotten episode in another lifetime, or book, at least ...

Hmm ... but, there was no error there in the script ... that was exactly what was happening ... so where had i gone wrong ? ... let's see now ...

★ Credit Card ★

The script was done like a bit sketch with no bite ... barely drawing a plot with nothing meaty to sink my teeth into ... no overture about the beginning ... hardly a trace of our intermission accomplished ... and The End was all in the pastel ... even the background mood was badly set ... it was only a paper moon, mooning a card board sky ... well, it wouldn't be make believe, believe me, if .. if ... it wasn't ...

But it was .. oh well, there's no matter in never a mind, i sighed ... but now, more importantly, hadn't someone once been saying something accusinglingly about *other characters* ... a limelight stealing Weasel ... and what a card ? ... but .. what a card was it that we were talking about ? ... i flashed the one that was held by my paw ... my Winning Card ... and t'was much to my credit, it seemt ... for no sooner had i done so than i heard a voice ... welcome, welcome, oh Weasel of the credit card ... some mysterious whom's voice welcomed me ...

31

★ A Leading (Prod) Question ★

Or was it a Whomette ? i wondered ... then the soft luxuriant voice spoke again .. with a prod ... now you Weasel .. (prod) .. what would you like ? .. (prod) .. it was like a leading question that lead me .. (prod) .. to the brink of a conclusion ... was i being .. (prod) .. lead around by the nose ? ... that would mean an whomette for sure, i surmised ... for whom else could be so ... so ... or ... (prod) .. so ...

Hmm .. i scratched a thought briefly as it surfaced near about my ears ... but it was brusquely .. (prod) .. prodded aside ... purr-chance you would like to .. (prod) .. browse a bit first, oh Weasel ? ... we have plenty of (prod) .. bargain buyables upon which to (prod) .. expend your winnings all over ... indeed, there were many items and a clock for sale that kept announcing cheep cheep ... just paw over your card, please ... she (prod) said ... and buy .. buy ...

Buy, buy ? .. Ah yes ... hello .. hello all ... i can hear you now questioning ...oh no it's Professor Weaselstein ! .. where have i been ? you wonder ... it has been so long since i was here last .. since i have been lecturing you about my ideas in persona .. but has it ? .. remember all the relatives ! .. if i had been traveling away at light speed, i could be back younger then you are now ! ... well, rest relaxed for a second or a long relative minute .. for i have been away delving in amongst the greatest question of existence ..The Big Bang Boom !! ... No No, my friends .. take an easy ... it happened along the time line a lengthy long while ago ... we are still only after-affecting it now ...but great unanswered questions were kaboomed upon us all back then ... you go figure, they said .. so i did, and now i'm back .. and what did i discover with my absence ? ... many maybes for sure ... and a few fine figures, too ...

For instant ... everyone is debating things like .. well, what really happened in the first zillionth of a split hair after the first second the Big Bang boomed ... whether in the second second and following seconds, lesser or Baby Boomers happened on purpose .. or whether it was an accident that no one really wanted ... was there an intelligent designer designing designs at work here ? .. or did things just evolve a bit on things's own ? ... now, now .. be quiet ! .. clamour down a bit .. this is important stuff .. you'll be glad to know that i have been able to discount *both* possibilities for sale to you now ! ..Yes ! No ! you say, but .. don't get so excited ... it is quite simple ... you see ...

And you *will* see ... but first we here at Weasel State College require a few courtesy account bytes of information ... hmm .. yes .. let's see .. name .. date of birth and/or expected expiration date .. and all Bank type information .. like your account number, for instance .. pass word ... and etcetera ... please send to :

    The Weasel Board of Directors
    c/o The Weasel Bored Group
    Over Education Road
    Under Skilled Pass out near Saint Weaselburg
    Newly Unified Weaslovakia .. Snouth Weast 37WE

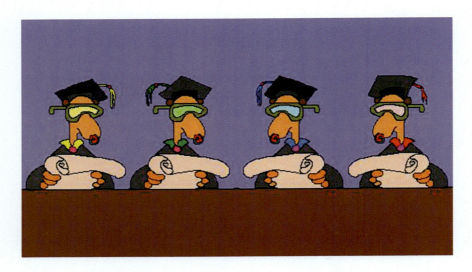

We will be glad to minimize your balance while we maximize our wallets ... and while we do this, please listen to and reflect upon the very important words that are flowing so eloquently from our very own mindful and very famous Professor Albutt Weaselstein ... thank you very with much heart felt gratitudes .. and gratuities, included ...

Okay ... we're back ... let's say for arguing land sakes alive, we take the first pointing view .. perhaps, maybe someone lit the Big Bang with a match or something in like flint .. or something whatevery .. whether this was *intelligent* per se is an whole another ball to wax about ... but let's say, it was done on purpose ... as if, somewhom had designs, per say ... but ! .. i per say ... then how do you explain Weaselettes ??? ... intelligent design ?? what ? where ? when ? whom ? how ? ... its a conundrummer drumming in the primeval forest ... see ? .. because .. with Weaselettes, in the equation which whom or what who could possibly argue *intelligent* anything ? .. whom, who or whatevernot ? ...

Well ... this was purretty obvious, i thought ... so i took upon myself some more thinking ... let's take a think on the second matter, i thank ... well, but then if things just *evolved* happily along their own way ... how can we explain Weasels ? ... quiet please ! ... now hear me out ! ... i have a scheme ... as we all know, the common Weasel in the woods hasn't evolved a smidgen since the twilights of existence exploded all over the place ... maybe it even was a Weasel in the fireworks that got the flint going to begin with ... and that could be considered pretty smart, going on brilliant ... but it was really kinder stupid, in a way too, eh ? ... since Weasels never learn and just keep blowing things and themselves up (and way out of portions, too, i would say) .. which isn't really bright, even though it is very flashy ... and this goes on right up to this day, as we speak ... see what i mean ? ... no intelligence ... *and* ... no evolvoultion ... Touché .. problem solved !

Well .. i would say that once again old Albutt makes some very excellent points, of course ... and we are all up to our ears in thank you debts of gratuities to him for it all .. but let's paradigm out a few more thoughts and give the ol' man's dice another toss ... taking the premises as premixed as follows .. 1) the very existence of the afore mentioned Weaselette implies without a doubt .. that there can be no intelligent design designed .. Fact ! .. and .. 2) the history of the Weasel undoubtedly concluses us to conclude .. that there is no evolution neither .. Fact ! ...

Startling and upsetting as this momentous discovery of these two self-evidential Facts is, we must all remain calm and clear headed in the right direction ... what, here, then, now, is it that is actually happening ? Professor Weasinberger, i would expect to hear you ask, then, here, now .. What ? ... well, let me tell you what ... i long deliberated many thoughts until i finally liberated a new one from them all ... which is as follows ... with Weasels and Weaselettes things just go round and round in circles forever ... it's all very quarky with ups and downs and strange charms ... and a lot of uncertainty, of course ... but, there's no intelligent evolution .. nor a easy way out to an end ... so that means we're left limboing in kind of a less than intellectual revolution ! ... yes, your ears heard correctly ! ... a *Revolution* is what i am proposing to suppose ! ... you may stop gasping now ... it is so very simple ... it is my theory of *Grand Circle Revolution* ... round and round as immortalized in my published collection of notes : <u>Of Weasels and Weaselettes</u> ... and we will come back around and around and around to it later again, i'm sure ... until then do your homework ... and think not what your Weasel can do you for, but ask what your tuition can do for me instead ..

Paw over my Card and buy buy !? .. not sooo fast Tootettes !! .. i thought with marks of propunctuation... there is nothing here of which i am in the dire needs of to buy ... why should i just paw over my card ? ... to her ?? ... after all the pickings and squabblings about that i had to go through to win it ... and always that whiny Author person constantly saying .. its mine, its is mine .. gimmmeee .. the Winning Card is for meeeee ... jeese ..

No my precious, i thought ... not this time .. it ... is ... mine .. i held it afar from reach ... and said .. oh .. so, you want me to paw over my card to you just like that, then ? ... she nodded ... i nodded ... i see, i said as if i saw .. to keep her off guard ... i nodded, again .. she nodded, again ... we're having quite a noddy time, i said, dodging a cheep lunge behind my back ... i gave her the old subtle behind the sunglasses Weasel wink which automatically changed the subject in mid-stream ... want to shuffle over to my place and do some real noddy stuff ??

Noddy stuff ? .. why you little Weasel ! .. i'll show you noddy stuff ! ... she answered resorting to a retort .. and nearly clonking me upon my nodkin with a lunge for my card ..

Well wonderful, i thought ... so much for *my* suggestion ... so what's your's ? .. what do *you* want to do ? .. i asked, thinking perhaps a shared glass of expensive fermentals could be in the picture ... but all i got was another cheep move ... my poor card ! .. i sighed .. and withheld it safely amiss ... whew, i was about to think .. when ...

★ A Notice I Noticed ★

When ... a unnoticed avenue of escape which had previously escaped my notice, no longer did .. for there, right next door to me .. i noticed and noted .. was a door ... and, as i noticed, i noted a note on the wall .. on the wall and hot pressed to be read, too ... but this notice was a note a bit unfocused to my eyes away over there ... i pawed it down and brought it on over towards my nose and mine closer eyes for so, oh, say, can to see .. in order to read ... now the wall was denoted and would remain not notable until someone noted it again .. but ..unnoticed, as i hoped i was, i noticed and noted this important fact, and .. oh, never mind ... i browsed upon it no longer .. but read on insteadily ...

You Weasel ! .. Give it to me ! ... it is mine ! ... i chose it ... I won it !!! .. i am the chosen one ... not you ! ... you ... you ... Weasel !

What was this .. then, again, now .. here upon this new juncture in time ? ... there was something all too familiar in the overriding lack of composure of this ... this ... poetry in motion ? ... was it iambic pentameter ? .. ironic stanza rima ? .. or just plain old far out beatnik ionic sphere ? ..

The Weasel, of course was the subject .. so .. it must be an idyl personified .. and most likely, the direct objection was the Weasel as well .. how clever, literally .. the *indirect* object was a little more or less subtle ... just hinted at, like a metaphor gone conclusion .. it might have been the Weasel .. or not ... an onomatopoeia quatrain refrain ? .. i could not contain myself .. for this was literacy just literally off the wall ! .. Author ! Author ! .. i shouted cheerfully, with a flip ... for i do so love cutting edge poetry ..

But had i not been thinking thoughts in the manner to which mine had grown accustomed to being thought ... i probably would have made some sense of them and denoted the danger of shouting so loudly and flipping out .. for no sooner had the Author escaped from my lips .. and all was echoing quiet while i landed ... than was i being delved upon with an alive performance of ...

Give it to me ! ... it is mine ! ... i chose it ... i am the chosen one ... not you ! ... you ... you ... Weasel !

Just like the original, i thought ... the plot was right on ... and the main character was still a real one ... i was reluctantly impressed ... but, still ... my problems seemed to be compounding unwanted interest exponentially ... first, there was the lingering cheepness .. and no fermented fruit juice ... what gives ? ... and then, that flipping Weaselette still after my winning card ... and then again, that irannoyitating Author whining about ... give it to me ! ... it is mine ! ... i *was* thinking about giving it to him ... with an all-new-this-episode-only-never-been-heard-before punch line ... when ...

When ... i renoticed the door ... when is a door not a door ? ... i mused ... when it's not knobby ? ... of course, without a knob you can't handle a grip .. it won't open ! .. its not a door ! ... wow, that's some thinking ... that would have taken a lesser Weasel forever to figure out ... but whomever never heard of a door not knobbed ? ... no one, of course ... but if it wasn't a door, then what was it ? ...

Well, it could still be an *exit* .. a avenue of escape ... i cautiously figured ... a door that's a avenue isn't really a door .. however .. davenue wasn't a familiar word quite ... hmmm, i was hmmming ... when the building noise constructed up the scaffolding to nearly a crescendo .. and distracted me from thinking ... that flipping Author was authoring up more bad Weasel lines .. Give it to mee !! ... and that pesky Weaselette was getting much too closely with her clutchy grasps ... and there was also some cheeping for a change of pecking order about whose hands held the Winning Card ...

★ Left Right Quickly ★

Enough of this ! ... i enuffed loudly .. and quick as aplomb, i reached out with the famous Weasel grasp of determination ... i turned the knob right .. which was wrong .. then left .. which was right ... then left right quickly ... i handled that pretty well, i thought ... for it *was* a door, it turned out ... it *did* have a knob to turn ... and it was my turn, after all ...

I slammed through ... then bolted it and down the hall ... on the other side of the wall ... a slammer on the go ...

★ Zippering Down the Davenue With Questions ★

So ... *this* is a davenue ? .. i thought with questions, while zippering down it ... thinking it was not exactly what i expected, was it ? .. but it had shown up right on the dime just within the nickel of time, hadn't it ? ... i could hardly have taken a minute more of that grabbing noise, could i ? ... and now .. i can't make any dollars out of what was going on here, can i ? ... everyone wants my winning card, don't they ? ... that's not part of the cricket, is it ? ..i thought, didn't i ? ... a game is a game, isn't it ? ... i chose the correct card to have been thrusted with, didn't i ? ... so, that should be it, shouldn't it ? ... game ? .. match point ? .. advantage Weasel ? .. match ? .. and strike out ? ... it was over, wasn't it ? ...finis ? ... khalas ? ... done well and well done ? ... i was victor, wasn't i ? ... i am victor, actually, aren't i ? ... but Weasel, too ...

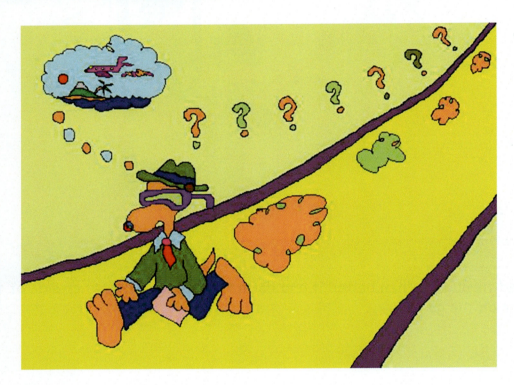

The world is full of poor spoiled sports, ain't it ? ... even though most spoiled sports aren't really poor, so to speak, are they ? .. otherwise they wouldn't be spoiled, would they ? .. just sports, huh ? ... that pesky Weaselette wanting me to exspend all my winnings on her ? .. and that Author ? ... how gauche, eh ? ... why should i put up with this ? .. perhaps i should take a vacation ? .. i considered ...

★ Pick A Card ★

Considering this idea was a new thought to me overall ... a vacation ? ... why yes ... i scuffled to a stop upon my bottom with this realization ... and shuffled through my ample deck of ideas ... a Winning Card ... plus mileage ... plus fair plane airfare .. minus lousy plain air fare (on the plane, there's never hardly a thing worth nibbling) .. plus a cute weaselette stewardess .. plus fine sunshine weather .. equaled ... one vacation ... it all made cognizant coherency cohere to my thoughts ... which was nice for a change, since nothing ever seemed to stick usually or lately ... this weary Weasel has been in the works too long, i figgered ... obviously, vacating to a break would be nice ...

But where to go to breakdown ? ... hmmm ... pick a card ... any card ... i thought .. before thinking, hey, wait a minuet or two, Miss Wall Flower .. i pondered a minute second ... these thoughts are sounding all too familiar ... firstly, i already did the "pick a card" Maitre dee thing .. secondly, i did the "pick a card" pick a card thing ... and picked a card ... the wining one ... already ...

45

Why should i do all this all again over ? ... some may say that i must .. for my card picking was rigged .. some might say that, also ... and some could say this, too ... may, might, or could ... but actually perhaps those some are all mistaken ... maybe, the card picked me, you see ... for after all ... it *was* a Wild Card ... and i was born to be a card ... put two and two together and .. hey ...

This born to be a wild card thing may or might or could have been fate ... i mean it may, might, or could be possible .. with a Weasel in the works anything is possible .. except the works part, of course ... but deep down outside my lack of blue sleighed shoes .. i suspected oranges and apples wouldn't give a lemon a lime over which hoot was which ... the realization rocked me like a stone on my foot ... ow .. wow .. that's pretty heavy, i thought ... that really curls my toes ! ... i kicked my full deck asunder and grasped my winning card with a gasp ... for i had just seen down my davenue a venue of what lay at the end of the road ...

An aerodrome of some kindly other ... and that .. that .. pesky Weaselette ... who gave no hoot but thought she was one ... a hoot ? .. my foot ! .. what a snoot .. i thought ... well, better play it closer to chess than the checkers .. i murmured .. stepping up to the counter and signaling to my chesty checker with the old Weasel demands Weaselette's attention finger gesture ... you there ! .. i began confidently, but slightly akimbo, for effect ... i want a ticket to ... to .. to .. ? ...

Oops ... i was standing in the already nearly gone line and didn't know where to ... exactly, go .. that is .. so, to speak, i ummed .. uummm ... where to go to ? ... everyone has always told me where i *could* go to ... but i wasn't overly interested in following their advice or suggestions ... a Weasel must think for himself, i thought .. or at least have a Weaselette do it for him ... got any suggestions ? .. where would *you* go ? .. i asked right on the cue, not missing a beating at all ... i don't give no flying hoot where you go ! .. she answered with disgruntle ... but ..i've got a Wild Card, you see, i said ... just give me your card !! she resnorted ...

Just .. just ... what ?!? ... i exclaimed questioningly ... i will speak very slowly so your furry little ears can seek the essence of what i am telling you, she answered, speaking very slowly .. presumably so my furry little ears could seek the essence of what she was telling me ... just between myself and my eye .. i didn't want to say anything, but it wasn't working ...

Give me your flipping card !! .. she demanded ... ah ha ! .. i reprimanded right back .. the Winning Card again ? .. ah ha, ha !! ..i responded as the essence of the matter sunk .. ah ha, ha ha !!! ... so that's was what all this holiday talk was about blowing smoke in my ears to grapple away my card ... i glanced an eye off my shoulder and caught a glint of yellow ... Trans Weasel Airlines ? ... i don't think so ... this was just a Cheep flight ...

And a cheep ploy too, i see and saw ... firstly, they would box me up the river in a flying crate ... secondly, they would tie me down to a time sharing package for shore after i was landed ... and finally, thirdly, they would abscoundrel away with my Winning Card, the pirates ! ...

This dismal projection ran flickering and jumped feature first as if off a tall billing .. would i be totally without credits ? .. my mind was in terminal oil .. slowly thinking into the gooey depths of despair .. what could i do ??

While i was worrying about these bad what-could-be's .. there came an interruptive elating soft lulling, lilting voice .. lifting like elevator music .. picking me up .. baggage ? .. it escalatored with each repetition .. Baggage ? ... this flipping airline, i thought ... i'll have a real suit case against them at this rate .. i'll sue .. it would be a brief case .. and they would owe me a bundle ..

I dropped thought suddenly .. what was this, anyway ? .. no one on my family tree ever traveled lugging luggage .. i mentally barked back my roots all the way up to when the last leaf left .. no baggage ... except ol' Freddy Ferret who was usually out on a limb .. he often ended up as a carry-on after a long wait at the terminal water hole ... my suspicions were arousing ...

When a ring rang a bell in my head suddenly .. Riiiing ... it wrangled loudly .. Boarding .. a very loud speaker was speaking .. please have your Boarding Card handy to hand into the eager welcoming greedy little paws of your friendly Cheep stewardette ... I was confused and pensive for a moment .. but quickly became expensive .. ah ha ! .. so that›s what this is all about .. i glanced through, up and around .. Boarding Card ? .. this wasn›t even a Cheep flight ...

The entire aerodrome was naught but a set set up for a setup .. an aerodrama was unfolding before me .. and would strike a rip off cord unless i bailed soon .. Boarding ? .. Pass ! .. i hollered .. and took off ...

★ In Flight or So ★

Down the runaway i flew ... destination, undetermined ... but determined to fly away ... i looked around .. whoa ... i was going up to around 30,000 feet an hour, at least, about .. at an average height of a foot per meter GMT .. or so ...

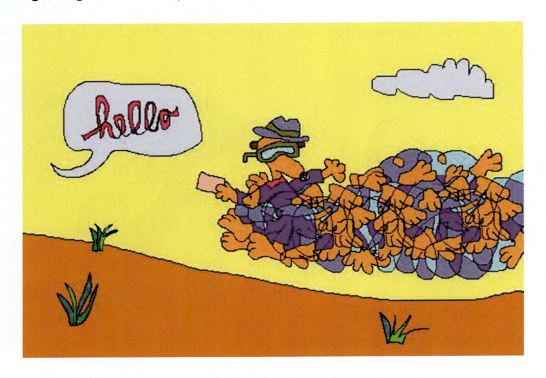

I heard a dong and a voice ... hello, welcome .. this is your Caption speaking, it said ... wow, i thought, i must just be flying off the pants of my seat to hear things like that ... if my Caption was speaking and i was hearing it .. then i was in flight along at at about the speed of sound, minimum .. or so ...

I figured that at this speed to slow down a bit would be a good figure ... so i did ... slimming down and trimming up a bit actually did make a difference .. but suddenly, i was startled out of my fine figure .. and noticed up ahead signs of trouble in the form of fat rolls of turbulence .. someone was standing smacking, dabbled and right in the midway of my flight plans ...

It was a Weaselette, of course .. what else ? ... but not just any brand ... this one was ... the Weaselette with Collidescope eyes .. and she had them in mind, it seemed for she wasn't moving out of the way ...

To collide at this speed ... well ... picture yourself in a train in a station with tangerines .. and you'll know just about how i felt ... i felt a shiver shiver right up my spine .. i say, shivery is not dead, like they say .. but i might be unless i start an immediate turnstile, i thought ... i applied some brake and screech before i plasticined a porter and became marshmallow pie .. i cellophaned left and taxied right to a fine state of non-motion ... a classical looking glass tie .. no winners ...

Out of the corner of my ear, somebody called me quite sweetly ... Yoo hoo Weasel ... i answered quite slowly .. for i sensed a being-tricked-out-of-my-Card-again moment was nigh on near ... Yoo hoo yourself Weaselette, i said ...

★ Shuffled Off ★

Well okay … it didn't seem like i was getting out of this one as easy as pie … even if it was supposed to be a cake walk … i stashed my card safely in pocket … You who? i repeated causally … since it was obvious i wasn't getting rid of this pesky weaselette, i might as well know which whom i was dealing with … she answered with an omnivalent silence … i decided to shuffle my thoughts …

But no matter how much shuffling i did, i kept coming up with the Winning Card … dang, i'll be accused of cheating forever … i worried briefly like a wart before formulating a plan of action … i'd already did the shuffle, so why not just scuffle away and be done with it? … it was a rhetorical question which needed no rhetorics … i shuffled off before you know who had a chance to cut the deck …

But this was getting to get a smidgen monotonous ... all these zipperings aways ... these flees in flights scenes ... i was the Weasel in the Works, after all ... it was me in the cards from the very beginning ... it was time to get back in the game and start weaseling things up a bit ... but how to do it ?

Let's see, i saw momentarily in recall ... once i was a Weasel without a cause, but now it was all different ... a) because it was, and b) because it is ... and see) because it was five card draw we were playing ... and d) as i recollected it ... i was supposed to be in the spotlight collecting it all ... i lit a josh stick from my pack of Weaselly Weasel Sniffs just for a laugh ... the fuming would help me concentrate ... nothing like a little simmering infuriation to temper things down for meditation purposes ...

And, yes … that brings us right back to all those things that were left to be picked up later … which now was now … i conjured down a bit for a moment from the mind … hmmm … i summoned a thought … a Weasel in the Works implies by ways and means that the Weasel works … which i knew by default is a fault of thinking … because, as i worked it out cleverly step by step, it was obvious: if i worked it out, then the weasel wouldn't have to … but i was he and he was me and i am altogether coo coo … achoo … so to speak … i sneezed from the josh … bless us one and all too …

For it was totally a contraddition … a Weasel in the Works, actually, isn't … a truly functioning weasel, actually, doesn't … actually, *can't* by definition … a weaseling workaholic, would quickly intoxify out .. which means a truly fine functioning Weasel couldn't actually function relatively speaking … there's actually a complex algebraic function somewhere that explains it all simpled down and log rhythmically … and as clear as an unambiguous bottle of laundry paradoxii … the Weasel in the Works didn't have to … which was the same as having the winning card … that wrapped things up pretty tidily, actually … it reminded me of that old saying "never use an aye for an eye before see, except after me" … and baby, that makes three …

And that old saying reminded me to get serious about things ...which seriously i often wasn't, as Vana used to imply with her "are you flipping serious Weasel ? are you *serious* ???" comments ... and i always thought i was ... geezit ... i would have to focus ... if you can picture that .. let's us see now ... just what does a Weasel in the works do when not in the works ? ... seriously ?

Well, relax for one, firstly .. get comfortable too, secondly .. then etceteraly, slip into the old nightgown type attire .. apply a layer of lap blankie .. expound upon a lounge chair .. practice a few casts ... hmm i could get used to this, i thought ... 'cepting that dang old fly was pretty hard to control and was flying around me and at will .. fairly embarrassing considering i tied it myself ... well, things could be and had been worse afore ...

So, i thought in theory ... our Weasel in the Works is purely an conjectural item-like thing ... a speculative ethereal entity ... which follows logically fine since some whom ... even if intangible, vague and elusive ... has to do the abstract work ... hypo-theoretically that is ... which is quite an interpretive problem in itself with work being so theoretical and all ...

Vana would call it idiotic, or more properly, *idiotique* ... however Vana wears glasses and has been known to be a bit short sighted ... her moments of lucidioticy are legendary ... i decided to get right down to "work" ... but only in theory, of course ... i stood up in my attire and diligently studied the Card on the fly which the fly had just caught on the fly ... for it was the cause of all these Weaselette problemas ... this Winning Card ... and yet ... it t'was of good weasel fortunes too ... which balanced the budget a bit ...

But first, we need a pause for sore sorry paws ... and we will be right back after this brief massage ... for mine are quite weary from all this intense paws on thinking type work ... and what could be better for paws than New Improved Weasolene ?? ... well, that's a difficult question answered surprisingly easily and stress-free ... Paw Lotion, for one, of course ... Paw Oil, two also ... Paw Spray-on Gloves are good, too ... lots of things really ... so if you are thinking of purchasing All New Improved Weasolene Eucalyptus Jeli for your paws .. well, don't bother ... it's quite expensive ... save your money ... for new scientific discoveries prove without a thought that Rubbing Dirt In'em will do just as well ...

Rubbing Dirt .. it's Grrrr-ate ... that's right !! ... don't be afraid to just rub it in ... why don't you ?? go on rub it in ... that's just Grrrrr-ate ... thanks a lot .. with friends like you, who needs enmity ?? ... this message is, was and always will have been brought to you by Planetary Earth Products Corps ... PEPC ... which includes a stunning inventory of clay, sand, fine and coarse gravel, mud and other variations of affordable dirt to match every purse ... so talk to your PEPC Rep and buy some today !! ... and get your filthy paws back on the ground ... all Credit and Winning Cards accepted ... Thanks forever after ... and now, back to the budget ...

The budget ? ... spending ? ... savings ? ... loans ? ... the gross and nauseating national product ? ... supply for demand ? ... gold ore break even points ? ... market basket observations ? ... upswings ? ... downward facing dog? ...geez, there was so much information ... i could almost ooze ... WEEP i thought ... this Work Ethic Etiquette Priority was invigorating ...

If i behaved properly and applied dynamic WEEP ... i could solve everything ... and more ... i was a little dewy eyed thinking about it all ... l'il ol' me ... entrusted to read 'em and WEEP ... but it was true, i had to start somewhere quite significantly ... and needs would have me to be very economic with my thoughts and/or my theories would get nowhere ...

★ Weasel Nomics ★

Ah ha ... economic thoughts ... very good ... i had much experience with economizing intellectual things like thoughts ... and every whom who contemplates such matters knows that to maximize the economy you have to minimize somewhere else ... thinking was a good place to start ... it's the karma balance thing in real time type action ...

And speaking of karma ... i recalled they were quite good at it in High Tidbit ... having mostly thought it up some time ago in their old books in them old temples and in those philosophic kind of old things they have over yonder ... perhaps i should outsource some of my more difficult thoughts to them there ... and then, call a hot line to find out what they are here ... that way I'd get 'em for half price ... then trade 'em on the open market ... milk the exchange rate and skim off the top ... while reaping the crème du la jour ... it was classic Weasel Nomics 101 stuff ... i read on through the night ... lapping it up ...

Thinking ... that that way i could internalize externally while externalizing internally before my competitors even got wind of it ... and by all accounts by banking my investments with derivatives i could even cash in the dividends into my savings deposits with extra fine securities ... bounce a few checks and watch it all roll over offshore somewhere ...

Add a little momentum and the process fluctuates eternally ... i had a gut feeling about this ... internally externalizing would be like poetry in motion sickness, in a general sense, of course ... but if i played my Winning Card right and kept it out of that pesky Weaselette's paws, i might not end up dispersing all my assets over the hedge fund ... i delved deeper into the matter as day broke and the lights went out ...

★ Information Overload ★

Wow ... this was some heavy stuff ... i thought it'd be easy to just cook the books a bit ... bone up on some knowledge ... then balance it all right out on the bottom line to be cool ... and call it a good day's night ...

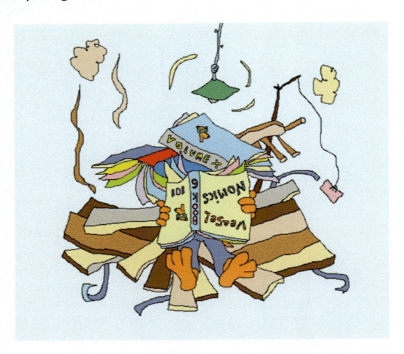

But it looked like information overload was upon me ... what an asymmetric systems shock ... consumption was converging in a dichotomy dumping of inelastic proportions ... yoy ... i was buried in extra volumes of interchangeable hypothecations ... the entire lump sum liquidity substitution was firming up to a new utility normative value and merging with network acquisitions at an endogenous pace ... fiscal drag was at a dangerous cyclic high ... i had a precautionary motive for optimum usury at this juncture ... but since it was all a bit fungible ... it crashed ... and boom went bust ...

All indicators were pointing towards an indifference curve of globalized proportions … that Weaselette again, i thought …i must keep a precautionary motive around such intangible assets seeking a competitive advantage with an effective transparency you could almost see through … i considered intervening with my invisible hand to boost some volatility of statistical significance … but figured such a standard deviation would cause unnecessary hysteresis … and i was already pretty sure of what my expected returns would be …

Enough speculation !! .. i reprimanded myself sternly … my eyes had already reached optimum oligopoly and were ready to pop out … dang her kleptocratic paws … i was feeling deflated and a bit depreciated … this Card withholding zero sum game was tiring .. there's just no equity in this world … but this was all regression analysis … i was getting nowhere … when suddenly an unbalanced leading indicator indicated a gap in the yield curve … follow the arrows, i thought … and did …

★ And I Was Out ★

And I was out in a heartbeat ... of there and away ... i held the incumbent advantage ... with Card in paw no less ...and no reserves about the long run ...

But .. it belongs to meeeee !!!! ... i heard a plaintiff cry ... what litigant dares accuses me ?? ... it must be Author again .. twixt this Author and that Weaselette my equilibrium will become unbalanced ... before i lose my quota i must abscond with myself tout sweet ... ere else my most favoured weasel status could be revoked and my misery index multiplier would be reciprocated heavily upon my portfolio ... no lagging now ... i went for broke ...

★ But Where To Oyster ? ★

And broke on through to the other side … but where to ? .. for except for my Winning Card, i was … broke … totally, but with a spirit unbroken … for as they say … and i like to remind the shop keepers … money cash in paw ain't everything … but alas as it turns out … it is … when you ain't got any …

But .. but … i am Weasel … i have the Winning Card, you see … whom needs money cash ??? … lookysee the New World is here … and it is my Oyster … but though they gathered about … and though they looked …none could see … for none saw it in the same manner into which i was accustomized to see it … and oyster or no, i was summarily ceremoniouslessly ushered away with a boot like a bum onto mine own … dust and pebbles flew …

★ Up Against the Wall Street Like a Rolling Scone ★

I got up and glimmered around a spell to see where about was my whereabouts ... and what about i could do about them ... ewe ... it was worse than not good ... this place where i stood ... i was up against a wall ... i was feeling so small ... like a flower without a pot ... like a dog not named Spot ... like a rose without a thorn ... like a rip that warn't actually torn ... like wood, fall, hot 'n horn ... like why not tie the rhyme up nicely and finish by working in all the solid platonic pentameter parameters into a truncated dodecahedron idyll jingle .. all alone ... with no direction home ... like a rolling scone ?

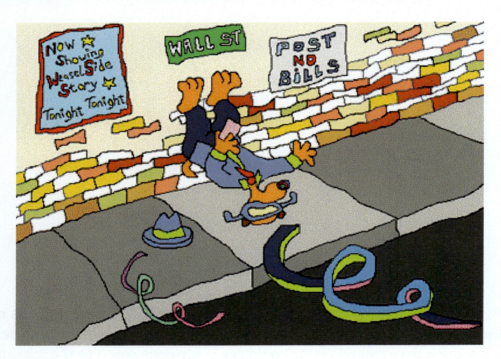

Well, probably not because ... since the butcher and the candlestick maker had just ejected me from the baker's heavenly gates of eatin' ... i was without dough but on a sourdough roll ... that ended up just another brick against this stone hedge and all ... on this street called Wall ...

Ah, hummed i to myself ... i have often walked down upon Wall Street before ... since i never had the taxi fare in my pocket and that's for sure ... and yes it's true, as i always knew, i was usually as high as the genetically modified corn seed in an elephant's eye ... knowing i'm on the street where i am ... oh that confined, closed-in, cramped-up and over-towered feeling ... seeing all the skyscrapers pressing at my nose ... and the Wall Street at my feet ... and .. and .. What? ... *that Weaselette reading the Deja views on the News ?*

Dag nabit wabbit ... all at once am i with several stories nigh on mixed up ... i flipped back a few pages .. let's see what story was this now ? .. and how did Vana get back innit ? .. Oh yes .. here it was, the lost thread ... yes, yes .. i was trying to do little ... so with a little bit of luck i wouldn't do more ... hmm ... but all this paper work .. i must be getting buried innit in the morning .. ding dong it all ... i moaned as i thumbed through my back pages ...

Wahl pilgrim, i said to myself, stoppin' walkin' .. we gotta do something significant .. i stashed my Winning Card into pocket .. and made myself a note .. i plunked another … then i plinked one more and let it fly .. "When in doubt break into a song" … that's what Old Great Grand Sing Sing Weasel used to say … and he had some real convictions about breaking into things … a true artiste he was .. they called him Ol' Buskin' Robin in the hood … come to think of it, his greatest hits happened right here on Wall Street where i stood standing on the corner .. with a flat B chord slowing down to make a B a A .. i placed my hat for tips strategically ..

Well, after all, i was very incorpsulated with doubt as to what significant thing to do .. so I went and followed the sing sing advice given and broke a nice verse to begin with … Oh give us a bone, i crooned … where the buffalo groan … and the dear old antelope play around like bulls and bears … where no one's ever heard … an intelligible word .. and no one's concerned … by whomever they burn … and the clouds are not cloudy in the day .. o .. day-ay-ay-o … daylights come knocking out and i wanna go hum … i was quite surprised of myself to be remembering all the song words so well …

★ Soy What Now - the New Order ? ★

I know .. i know .. i know all the words ... that's what i said ... i said ... now hear me out ... i said ... stop repeating me, i said ... and hear me out ... and that's what i said ... i said ... i said that already ... i said that's what i said ... stop repeating me ... i said again repeating that's what i said ... echo tango, Charlie ? .. i protested .. but this wasn't a protest song .. i sighed and curbed my guitar and sat ... at this rate i'd never break the chain ... i felt so small and whelmed over by it all .. even my last note to myself was gutter sniping off ..

Soy what now ? ... i thought I could milk this for all it was worth .. but in the end .. cow paddy cake it all .. it was the same old tune .. and weed bin down that road before .. it was time for new directions on the horizon .. i glazed off into the future and decided if it would be wise to bank on the New Order ..

Why sure .. why not ? .. let's see .. thistle be simple .. all i would just need to do is recruit some weasels from the Weasel World Bank … and incorporate some real thought type thinking .. and make a devious twist .. i'll sue all the countries who sign up with me .. a ha ha .. and .. fulfill my destiny of maximizing profiteering .. one small step for Weasel .. one giant step for Weasel World domination !!

First of all the alls i'd have to do is to get on board with the Trans Specific Weasel Partner Ship .. and the Transweaslantic Investment Part Nerd Ship .. and then get cozy with some International Trade Weasels Agreements .. and then per consequences .. i would toss in some revolving back door transactions .. get polluted in an environment or two .. steal some jobs and ship them offshore with my taxes as crew .. appoint myself as Chief Head Operational Weasel In Charge (CHOWIC) .. write myself a few healthy bonuses .. then tack on a vigorous cost-of-living-well allowance .. toss in hearty perks and hale raises .. and all will be honky donkey for definite sure … smooth sailing all the way .. this would be like a piece of haggis for a clever savvy salty Weasel dog like moi self .. i would be right smacking in the works without having to be doing any to speak of ..

I went nobally up to the door knob of the Weasel World Bank and rapped authoritatively upon its knockers .. it is i, i announced when the door opened a crack and i popped myself inside .. i showed them my Card ..

I am known, by George .. and by a pesky Weaselette too .. to verify, just look up Weasel at the local library or follow me on-line on Visage Livre .. would you like to be my friend ? .. i'd like to be your friend ..

We could play Parcheesi .. and have snacks .. i'll bring the Par and you can be Cheesy ... i glanced at the menu .. i looked at my feet .. one .. two .. three .. oh four crying out loud .. said i .. i lack toes .. cheese just wouldn't cut it at all .. sorry .. i'd like to place a New Order, i said meekly ..

★ The 99.00001 Percent Dream ★

I notably refer myself to you with much excellents, i said when the New Order was straightened out .. Cacao not Cocoa Puffs please .. i placed myself upon a quietly coloured chair in the waiting room and handed the menu back to the waiter .. from waiter to waiter, see you later .. i thought .. till dusk do us part .. i got back to business .. i am the 99.00001 percent .. which, as you can see, puts me a step over the line .. into elite .. it's all documented in books and things ..

And not only that .. i have a Dream .. i do ... or at least i did last night actually that was really really weird .. you can't imagine .. i was walking along a crowded street and people were pointing and girls were giggling and i felt a breeze and i looked and saw i warn't wearing any .. oh .. but this is way besides it all and off the point .. please allow me to snap back ..

I looked around my now snappy loud coloured chair and immediate environs .. i was in a very huge enormous staring at an Occupied desk .. many characters had recently made vast hauls from this vast hall, i realized .. and then got away with it .. How .. i said for intros using the old 'Merican native greeting from the cowboy movies .. i raised my paw in the proper manner .. How .. how did they get away with it ? .. how did they do it ? ..

Yes yes yes how ?? .. how did they do it ?? .. how ? .. i want to do it tooooo ... tell meeeee .. tell meeeee .. it's is all mine anyway .. like the Card .. give it to meeee ..

What's all this ?? .. blue letters ?? .. that Author again ? .. where did he come from ? .. go away .. vamoose !! .. scram ! .. scat ! .. shoo ! .. skedaddle !! .. go ! .. and git too ! .. now where was i now ? .. oh yes .. How ..

I demanded to see the Chief High Executive Whom In Cahoots (CHEWIC) .. i could do this since i had recently been self-anointed CHOWIC myself .. i wish to employ some of your WWB Genetically Mollified Organisms for a futures plan of great significant magnitudes .. i wish to reach for the stars .. i wish to wish upon a star .. i wish to swish my magic Card and stare at the stars staring at me ..

No .. no i'm serious, i said seriously .. but first i'll need some of your GMO's to work on the toxic hedges .. we'll get all the bugs worked out .. and your GMOs will convince them to commit pesticide .. trust me .. i know how this works .. even if i don't .. work, that is .. now please .. i'd like to see the CHEWIC .. but first my Cacao Puffs ..

Cacao Puffs ?? .. did i hear correctly ?? ... meeee tooooo ... i want Cacao Puffs tooooooo ...

CHEWIC showed up promptly on a dime for she .. (she?? i thought alarmed) .. had heard it was CHOWIC cum Card who beckoned a call .. i was pensive and a bit aprespensive too .. for no CHEWIC has never ever .. to my knowledge .. ever ever shown up immediately upon a beckoning from a CHOWIC .. for such a transgression of form has never happened .. i checked my old coarse memories from Weasel State .. History of Executive Type Weasels - Issues 101 .. nope .. never happened ..

Except for maybe that time when CHEWIC was a little sick .. and CHOWIC was under the weather also and not really summoning a beckons whole heartedly .. thence they just got on the telephone immediately .. whence CHEWIC explained to CHOWIC why CHEWIC couldn't visit CHOWIC at that moment .. and CHOWIC was very understanding about what CHEWIC was saying about not visiting CHOWIC since CHOWIC and CHEWIC had mutual compatibilities of harmonious goals .. which were out of the harmony due to sickness .. nevertheless CHEWIC and CHOWIC ended up chewing the fat for some time and agreed to make amends over chow sometime later .. which they never did since CHEWIC is usually busy when CHOWIC is free .. and the vice verse is true for CHOWIC too .. but officially they thought to chew chow sometime together would have been a good idea .. and subsequently they said so in speeches .. but that was many years ago ..

Me too .. meeee tooooo ... i wanna chow tooooooooooo ... give me the Card so i can chew chow tooooooo ....

Yes .. yes yes .. and yes again .. i remember it as if it were just some time ago .. which it apparently was .. well no matter .. i had signed on with Weaselco da Gramma Tours to sail the world's seven seas .. well .. really maybe just one or two of them actually .. never mind .. so how surprised i was to discover that Weaselco was in reality a Weaselette .. da Gramma, she was .. ar .. and an old gal she was too .. and her idea of wide world exploring was searching for new embroidery patterns and stitching twills .. when she started on her old yarns about synthetic crocheting, weaving in and out of buttonholes, selvedges and weft warps .. i knew i was in trouble .. this was not the millinery vacation for me .. i felt like ruching into a placket .. my templates ached .. i hemmed ribbons off my haberdashed spirits .. i was piping and up in armscyes .. my gusset flared many pleated gores .. my eyelets interfaced with frilly ruffled braids .. godet baste it all !! .. i crocheted loudly .. and darn it too !! .. but what could i do ?? .. what would a grommet do ? .. my contract was binding .. quilting in the middle of a journey was not my style .. knitting the whole tail together would mean braiding an applique of fusible patchwork .. before i unraveled .. what a placket .. i had been upholstered .. i should have stayed in Textiles .. only a seam ripper could save me at this petticoat junction ...

Or was there something else ?? .. it was a big surplice .. but .. low and beholden all was not lost .. for wisely i had earlier purchased Around the Horn Travel Insurance .. yes .. yes yes .. and yes again, again .. on one hand was disaster and on the other hand was my tried and true No Money Down Percentage Plus Policy with Turnover Compatibility and Total Recurrence .. our special Open Parachute edition for when all your dreams are dashed and down you come with an overlock knot stitch that has you thimbled into a toile .. all is not lost .. no indeed, all is not lost .. but only if you have purchased our tied and true

Ultramarine Blue Pre-Leveraged Full Body Coverage Around the Horn Travel Insurance ..
Still available at bellbottom package prices if you act now !! .. so don't be a gimp .. weave
on down over here to AtHT Insurance with Card or Money in hand .. and purchase to buy
a little trim and add a safety pin to your travels ..

For Full Coverage Sunblock Travel Insurance

Please Send all your money to:

The Weasel @ AtHTI - Tahiti
Bora Bored Walk by the NAPS 324 PM every afternoon
Mid Pacific Ocean Blvd.
Bora Board Island
French Toast Coast
Somewhere Over the Sea

Credit Cards are exceptional (if valid).

Thank You Merci Much

Well .. since O comes before E except in the alphabet and in geologistics .. and i being CHOWIC with an O and all .. well, i began the big CHEWIC-CHOWIC Information Technology C2 IT summit discussion with the usual "well" ... Well, i have hitched my star Card onto some strange ships in the past .. but these Part Nerd Ships are in all my days at the freely traded bazaar the most bizarrest .. CHEWIC nodded as if she understood what i was talking about .. which she couldn't have .. since i didn't .. i continued .. Well, for first of all the balls off the bat .. these Ships don't make cents for anyone but the big corporate anonymous rat types .. Well, and maybe also for the lesser anonymice too, i suppose ... Well, and even they are just worried about the dollars .. Well, so .. no sense are included ...

Well, i said .. my dear CHEWIC .. for your Info Tech only ... IT is a strange business altogether now, because if you join in a Part Nerd Ship ... Well, then they can do whatever they want you to do .. technogollically speaking .. Well, you'll be like an informed stowaway .. if you're a part nerd of the ship who cares what happens to you ? .. Well, you'll be oppressed into service like a colonial .. Well, that's because they can get Sue onto you too .. if you do anything to worry their profits .. Well, then they'll say you're being, by cricket, illegal .. Well, yes .. that's a whole new ugly suit with buttons inclusive .. and Well, you know .. Well, i could have Welled on forever .. but by the wholly profit !! .. i was stirred into a humble by speaking so Well to CHEWIC .. who simply said .. Well well well, what's with all the fracking "Wells" anyway ? .. oh and is that your Card? .. and shouldn't it really be mine ?? .. nope .. i responded quickly looking at it closely .. my card's not on the table for examination .. so I'll table that suggestion toute .. Well, we a-hemed and we a-hawed for a while longer as usual to fill up our allotted budget .. as day fell into evening .. while i kept yonder Card from yonderess's paws .. and then we called it good .. and of course .. Well .. for the night ..

Well, we wrapped up the C2 IT meeting quickly since it was already past hours .. and i didn't want to get Carded .. because the way i thought about IT had to be thought anonymously and not on public placards .. since there is so much stigma attached to thinking nowadays .. ol' Grumpy Gramps used to say "think not; want not" .. and it is the best advice i have ever .. uh .. ever .. evered ..

But it was useless as ever trying to follow such sageous advice .. i could not think not .. for i was presently pre-occupied .. and couldn't keep my mind shut .. or mouth neither .. every time i opened it .. out came .. Occupy .. because it was always occupied speaking ... so instead, i entered it on the key board .. i hit Save and headed for relief ..

★ Occupied ★

But when i went to the Weasel's Room .. it was already occupied .. i thought under the circumstances i could nip into the Weaselette's .. butt that was occupied too .. the reception desk was still all so occupied .. and now my chair was occupied on top of it likewise by some weasel else who sneaked in while i was occupied .. i got on the phone and called my Senator Snout on the Weaslonian Capitol Hill to complain .. but the line was occupied .. dang .. everything's occupied, i fretted .. the 99 percent already got it all .. this was not right ..

I made a bolt for the exit door before someone could affix a bolt and bolt me in .. and put me to work on some Transweasel Part Nerd Ship ..

★ Check Out Stand ★

But House Land Security had already set up a checkout post .. and before i could leave with my Card, i had to go through with it .. and going through with it would not be easy i knew .. for it was a well sought after Card which i had won .. and it would undoubtedly beep ..

Won ?? .. you won ??!! .. you beep !! .. it's is mine i tell you .. all mine .. meeee .. i won it !!

I swiped MY Card at the check-out stand .. but it didn't take .. so i swiped it again .. but it still didn't take .. dag it .. i punched in my password .. no takers .. digit all .. someone must have taken it, i thought .. someone swiped it !! .. what to do ??? .. my Winning Card was useless .. i was taken aback in the given situation .. there was nothing for it else .. i would have to tear it up !!! .. i would have to execute an immediate execution decision .. my mind's eye heard a CHEWIC say .. don't you dare you flipping stupid Weasel .. don't you dare .. i have chased after hither with dithers for it .. and now all i need is your new password .. do not be tearing the Card up !! .. but it was too late .. my head's ear saw another voice .. it was that Author ..

Execute ? .. Tear it up ?? .. Whaaaaat ??? .. you can't !!! .. it's is mine !! .. mine i tell you … miiiiiiinnnneee … give meeeee it … gimmmmeee !! .. i won it fairly square !!! .. you cannot be tearing it off into shreds !!!

Well to make a short story shorter .. my decision conflaggerated in a blink .. i tore up my Winning Card and punched myself out .. i heard a mournful whale .. like the sonars of them ol' wails of the watery ocean blues .. it bubbled and frothed loudly and dwindled like the settled sun woefully thinking over the next horizon ..

NOOOOOOOOOOO !!! .. Nooooo .. nooo .. no .. nooooooooooo ……. o ..

The whines intermangled with a muffled mutter sputtering something about .. NOW i have HAD it up to my nose with that Weasel !! .. i'm going home .. i'm finished .. i'm done with all iddy okra weasels !! .. i think that was it .. or was it well done audio ochre whistles ? .. idiotic wattles ? .. itty autocratic wiggles ? .. it was difficult to understand in the heat of the circumstances .. i broke onto the other side ..

★ Outside ★

I was outside .. and correspondingly out of work .. and the Works, also .. had i really weaseled it all the way through another book ? .. there was not an anything anywhere about a Weasel in the Works .. i looked all around myself .. nowhere up .. nowhere down .. nowhere all around the town .. Hooray !! .. i hoorayed .. i worked it all out once again .. i was away .. and free ..

Me tooooo ... me toooo .. i am free tooooo ... no more writing about dummy dim whittled dumb Weasel .. no more me in the Weasel Book Works either !! .. i never wanted stupid Winning Card anyway ...

Go away stupid Author .. said i with finality ..

Ah .. once more we have arrived at long last to that happy-sad magical Book End moment ..
how it sneaks upon us all with so little warning .. without no fanfare nor big production ..
no nor hullabaloo tumult or ballyhooing to mark the shemozzle end of another kerfuffle
of marvelous Weasel Episodes .. which are now all wrapped up for you very nicely in a
tidy well-earned Book End Calm For Nano Weasolene .. yes, after all the exciting pages
have flipped on by .. and now when there ain't no more flipping weasels for you to flip ..
a Panic can be predicted anxiously .. i mean what else can you expect to follow happily
apres ever after ?? .. PANIC .. Yes, but panic not my friends for after so much vicarious
Weasel viveocracy has rushed around through your veins building up adrenaline through
all those episodes .. well, one's blood naturally boggles with aspirations of calm calmness ..
it's only natural to want calmness now .. Yes .. well, that's all good and well .. but calm
comes to you only if you are fortified with a fresh prescription for All-New Wonder Nano
Weasolene .. it is an absolute Wonder .. for even your Doctor is still wondering about this
Marvel of Miracle Phenomenonical Products .. for it comes in all forms of Nano Particle
Presences .. Cremes, Rubs and Sprays .. all of which are fabricated of only the finest
rare wee miniscule tiny particles ... that are regrettably Invisible .. Yes you heard right ..
totally Invisible .. this causes many user doubts .. but you must not doubt no longer ..
believe us .. Nano Weasolene really is there .. you can't touch it .. you can't feel it .. you
cain't hear or smell it .. and it's completely tasteless ... So you may be tempted to say Na
! No !! .. Nano Weasolene just ain't there ..

But it is .. and ... it will bring an eerie intangible calm to you and your bank account .. and
that my friend is tangible ..

So wait no longer - there is only the Awards presentation left in this tail - and try one of these amazing Nano products .. take your pick from the table .. be careful .. we don't want to spill any ... one sample per patient please .. yes they are on the table .. then if you are satisfied .. or even if you're not .. you can buy plenty more .. for more please see the Contract below ...

Contact for Contract :

Dr. P.H. De Weaseling
M.D. of Weasolene Studies
M.S. of Much Stuff and Matters
B.S. of All Matters
Honorary Fellow of Mutual Symbolic Symbiotic Substances
Vice Associate and Consultant too to Clinical Quacks Inc.
Cum Laud

@

Dollars Or Cents DOC
142 Penny Lane over Chagrin Way
New West Weasolopolis
Near Weaselton

Thank You

Your invisible Nano Prescription will be sent to you upon
confirmation of your Visible Bank Assets

★ And Now ★

Yes .. and Now .. it is now again time for the Finale .. we apologize for the greyness of the hour .. but so much was going on .. and bills were not paid .. and the electricity company is so impatient .. and .. and .. well never mind .. here is the formal presentation of the Book Six - Nearly Original Weasel Award Cup .. All New this edition only .. and completely different from what you have received any time earlier for finishing from first page to last each Weasel Chronicle storybook .. this for gumption is an All Nearly New Weasel Classic Occasion !! .. yes .. this is classic indeed .. for on top of your NOW Award Cup you will receive the following Bonuses :

1) An entire year's supply of Complimentary Compliments

2) Twelve months of Second Day Certificates

3) Twelve Indorsed Days of 24 hours each

4) A life-time subscription to Weasel Boy e-mails with all fold-outs inclusive

5) A penny for your thoughts

6) A handshake with three fingers, one thumb and a palm

Yes, you will receive all or nothing of these bonuses over, above and on top of your basic NOW Reward Cup .. this means you will get to choose from Nearly to Mostly to Actually Nothing of the items above .. and with no extra charge ($) you will also receive your Basic Weasel Rewards Package including e-packaging and virtual ribbons

Thanks So Much

And Weasel All See You Next Book

Why?

Because We Love You

And Your Influential Assets

Remember Be HAPPY Tomorrow
For Today It Might Rain !

Op. Cit.

★ Epilogue – And So, Life Was Good.. ★

So, the Awards had all comest to have been awarded. The Weasolene had all been dispensed. Happiness reigned upon the brows of all concerned. But still, closure was earnestly knocking on those brows to tie the story ends up like in traffic.

So, Author collected himself and went home. With his new found experiences in hand, he sat down to pen some more words. In the end, he penned a Best-Selling Novel creating for himself a Winning Card, for with to live Happily Ever Afterwards. Life was Good.

So, the Weaselette took herself, also, home, but, in a huff. She puffed down before the television, pulled down the shades and imbibed in Cooking Shows. In the end, she made an uneducated guess about a recipe on a quiz show and won a nice plastic-like Card. It was a Winning Card, and so she was Content Forever Afterwards and didn't hoot about what the stupid Weasel did. Life was good.

So, our poor weary Weasel, also, also, meandered home. Fairly happy with the outcome of the story, he sat at the counter and fiddled with his deck of cards. Flipping through, card by card, until there, upon the scene, arrived a brilliant realization. "By Gum," he said ... "Every deck of cards has two Weasjokeler Cards!!" And there it was. He stood up and quietly pocketed his new Winning Card out of Weaselette sight and pesky Author ... He whistled a happy tune. Life was Good.

So, Happiness and Contentment fluttered about in the air as the adventures wound down to end again, but this time a Moral popped up like a rodent. "Don't gamble too much, deal the cards with the hands you're dealt, and you'll live content and happily ever after – until something else comes along to play 52 card pickup and scatters the deck again." Life is Good.

Fin

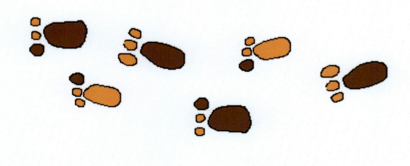